THE HISPANIC INFLUENCE IN THE UNITED STATES

LATINOS
IN AMERICAN HISTORY

HERNANDO DE
SOTO

BY JIM WHITING AND KIMBERLY GARCIA

Mitchell Lane
PUBLISHERS

P.O. Bo
Bear, Delaw

THE HISPANIC INFLUENCE IN THE UNITED STATES

LATINOS
IN AMERICAN HISTORY

OTHER TITLES IN THE SERIES

Visit us on the web: www.mitchelllane.com
Comments? email us: mitchelllane@mitchelllane.com

THE HISPANIC INFLUENCE IN THE UNITED STATES

LATINOS
IN AMERICAN HISTORY

HERNANDO DE
SOTO

BY JIM WHITING AND KIMBERLY GARCIA

Printing   1   2   3   4   5   6   7   8

Library of Congress Cataloging-in-Publication Data

Whiting, Jim, 1943- and Garcia, Kimberly, 1966-
        Hernando de Soto/Jim Whiting and Kimberly Garcia.
        p. cm. — (Latinos in American history)
        Summary: A biography of the wealthy Spaniard who came to the New World to seek glory and who, in 1541, became the first European to cross the Mississippi River.
        Includes bibliographical references and index.
        ISBN 1-58415-147-1 (lib bdg.)
        1. Soto, Hernando de, ca. 1500-1542—Juvenile literature. 2. Explorers—America—Biography—Juvenile literature. 3. Explorers—Spain—Biography—Juvenile literature. 4. America—Discovery and exploration—Spanish—Juvenile literature. [1. Soto, Hernando de, ca. 1500-1542. 2. Explorers. 3. America—Discovery and exploration—Spanish.] I. Title. II. Series.
E125.S7 G09 2002
970.01'6'092—dc21
        [B]   2002022142

ABOUT THE AUTHOR: Jim Whiting has been a journalist, writer, editor, and photographer for more than 20 years. He has edited more than 20 titles in the Mitchell Lane Real-Life Reader Biography series and Unlocking the Secrets of Science. He is the author of several biographies for young adults, including *Francisco Vasquez de Coronado* (Mitchell Lane.) Kimberly Garcia is a bilingual journalist who found her first job at a newspaper on the U.S.-Mexico border because she spoke Spanish. Her paternal great grandparents migrated from Spain in the early 1900s. Garcia has a bachelor's degree in English and Spanish literature from the University of Wisconsin in Madison. She is the author of several biographies for young adults, including *Lance Armstrong* and *Janet Jackson*.

PHOTO CREDITS: Cover, Getty; pp. 6, 9, 12, 18, 22, 30, 34, 38, 40, 43 Northwind Picture Archives; pp. 21, 24, 36 Corbis.

PUBLISHER'S NOTE: This story is based on the authors' extensive research, which they believe to be accurate. Some parts of the text might have been created by the authors based on their research to illustrate what might have happened years ago, and is solely an aid to readability for young adults.

        The spelling of the names in this book follow the generally accepted usage of modern day. The spelling of Spanish names in English has evolved over time with no consistency. Many names have been anglicized and no longer use the accent marks or any Spanish grammar. Others have retained the Spanish grammar. Hence, we refer to Hernando de Soto as "de Soto," but Francisco Vásquez de Coronado as "Coronado." There are other variances as well. Some sources might spell Vásquez as Vázquez. For the most part, we have adapted the more widely recognized spellings.

CONTENTS

De Soto landed off the coast of Florida, possibly near modern-day Tampa Bay on May 29, 1539. Several days later, when all his men and horses had made it ashore, he claimed the land in the name of the Spanish crown. The first of de Soto's vessels to approach Florida was a Spanish brigantine. A brigantine could be either sailed or rowed. They were small, light galleys used for exploration in shallow coastal waters and rivers like the one you see in this picture.

THE BATTLE OF MABILA

Hernando de Soto (Air-NON-doe day SO-toe) was feeling pretty good as he sat, relaxed, ate and drank his fill and watched a group of Indian women singing and dancing for him and a small group of his soldiers. It was a mid-October morning in 1540, and the Spaniards had just arrived in Mabila, an Indian village in what is now the state of Alabama.

While it had been more than a year since de Soto had landed in Florida, and he still hadn't found the gold and silver that he was expecting during a march of more than 1,000 miles, things had gone well the past several months. Despite some earlier fighting with the Indians, especially as his 600-men army made its way through Florida, his losses had been minimal. His men were equipped with the latest European weapons, and this armament, combined with their massive horses, gave the de Soto expedition a huge advantage over any Indians who tried to oppose them. Every time they entered a new village they would force its leaders to accompany them. They would also draft the villagers to carry their baggage, often chaining them together in a long line. Frequently they would demand young women, too. This system worked well—for the Spaniards.

But de Soto might not have felt so good if he had known what was taking place just a few yards away. The cacique, (kuh-SEEK) or chief of the local tribes, a huge man named Tascalusa, was meeting in a hut with other tribal leaders. They were deciding how best to kill their visitors.

De Soto had had some clues that pointed toward danger. Several days earlier, two of his men had been killed by local Indians—the first deaths due to hostile action in nearly six months. Then he sent scouts riding ahead to inspect Mabila while the rest of the men followed slowly behind them. The scouts returned with ominous news. Hundreds of armed men were pouring into the town. Many others were reinforcing the palisades, or the walls that surrounded the town. In addition, they had cleared the land just outside the walls.

But de Soto ignored the warning signs. He told his alarmed officers that he wanted to sleep in a house, not in the open. Besides, he wanted to appear confident in front of the Indians. Doing anything else might be interpreted as a sign of weakness. On top of everything else, he had a 25-year string of almost unbroken successes in the New World which had made him one of the richest men in Spain after beginning as an almost penniless teenager. But his overconfidence was to cost him dearly.

The day had started out as he had expected. Riding inside Mabila's walls at the head of perhaps 20 or 30 men, with the rest of his army strung out for several miles behind him, he was welcomed with music, showered with gifts and escorted to a place of honor in a small plaza in the center of the town.

This hand-colored woodcut shows a Native American village within palisades similar to the Indian town at Mabila.

Tascalusa excused himself and joined the other local chieftains to plan their tactics. Some wanted to attack immediately. Others wanted to wait until the rest of the army had arrived. They decided not to wait, so hundreds of concealed warriors poured out of the houses. Several Spaniards died almost at once, but de Soto and the rest of the surprised men made their way to safety outside the walls.

Then the Mabilians urged the hundreds of Indian porters, who were waiting just outside the walls with all the supplies, to join them inside. The unhappy men didn't need much encouragement, and rushed inside carrying the baggage. As soon as they were inside the walls, the Indians shut and locked the gates.

De Soto rallied the men who were nearby. He ordered them to surround the town to keep any Indians from escaping, then as more men began arriving he divided them into four different troops to attack the town and break down the walls.

The battles continued through the rest of the morning and then into the afternoon with more and more Spanish reinforcements appearing. Finally they smashed down the walls in several places, and men poured inside and began setting the houses on fire. Hundreds of Indians were burned to death or smothered. Many more escaped the flames, only to be cut down by Spanish lances and swords. As more and more of their men perished, Indian women took up bows and arrows.

But it was to no avail. The battle finally ended at sunset.

We don't know how many Indians died. Those who participated estimate between 2,500 to 11,000, though to showcase their own bravery—and cover up for de Soto's overconfidence— they may have inflated the totals.

Whatever the amount, it was a devastating blow. Most of the fighting men from an important tribe that probably went back for several centuries perished. Less than 20 years later, another Spanish expedition found only a handful of survivors. For the Indians, the Battle of Mabila was the end of a civilization.

While it wasn't the end of de Soto's expedition, the battle was a crippling blow. At least 20 men were killed during the battle, with more dying later. De Soto suffered two personal losses. His son-in-law, Don Carlos Enríquez, was killed early in the fighting. Later in the day his nephew, Diego de Soto, was shot in the eye with an arrow as he tried to avenge the death of his brother-in-law and died the following morning. More than 200 Spaniards were wounded, including de Soto himself who suffered a painful arrow wound in his hip. Because they had no medical supplies, the one surviving surgeon and his helpers had to cut open dead Indians and use their body fat as salve for wounds.

The expedition lost many horses, a serious loss because of the huge edge that the mounted Spanish cavalry enjoyed over their opponents. Even more serious was the loss of virtually all of the army's baggage in the fire. That included food and clothing, extra weapons, everything that was needed to say the Catholic mass, and several hundred pounds of pearls, the one tangible sign of wealth that they had discovered so far.

And worst of all, the battle forced de Soto to make a decision that from our vantage point more than 400 years later was the wrong one. It doomed an expedition that still might have been successful. And it cost him his life.■

This is a portrait of Hernando de Soto. Not much is known about de Soto's early life, but historians have been able to put bits and pieces together.

CONQUISTADOR'S CRADLE

Historians don't know much about Hernando de Soto's early life, but they believe that he was born between 1496 and 1500 in the south central Spanish province of Extremadura. He was one of at least four children born to Francisco Méndez de Soto, a poor Spanish nobleman, and Leonor Arias Tinoco in the town of Jerez de los Caballeros.

De Soto's family came from the military class which had been created to fight a long war against the Moors, who were Muslims from Northern Africa. They invaded Spain at the start of the 8th century and were gradually expelled during the following 700 years. His earliest known ancestor, Méndez Sorred, was a captain under Alfonso IV, the king of the Spanish province of León in the early 10th century.

De Soto's father was among the minor nobility in the Méndez Sorred lineage. De Soto's mother, who came from Badajoz, the capitol of Extremadura, was descended from a more important family that included attorneys, administrators and military officers. The two married in the 1490s, and had at least two sons, Juan Méndez and Hernando, and two daughters, Catalina and María.

The de Sotos lived among 8,000 people in Jerez de los Caballeros, a walled area of less than one tenth of a square mile. Living conditions were unpleasant in tiny, cramped homes along a maze of narrow streets overrun with dogs, chickens and goats feeding on garbage and feces. Most people spent their time outdoors, either in gardens or in one of three open plazas. The largest plaza faced the church of San Miguel that de Soto attended as a boy. A strong and active black-haired youth, his favorite activities were engaging in mock duels on foot or horseback and exploring the nearby river and ruined castle.

But de Soto would not remain long in his hometown. The world at large beckoned his adventurous spirit. Christopher Columbus had discovered the Americas in 1492, and Spain teemed with stories about fame and fortune gained in the New World. De Soto's life in Jerez de los Caballeros seemed much less promising in comparison to the stories. He was the second son of the family, so his older brother would inherit the family's meager possessions. His parents hoped the youngster would pursue a religious or educational career, but he showed more interest in tales of chivalry—stories about knights in shining armor—than in academics.

So one day in his early teens, probably in 1513 or 1514, de Soto set out for Seville, the departure point to the New World. Don Pedrarias Dávila, one of King Ferdinand II's most trusted military leaders, had recently been named governor of what is now modern-day Panama. Vasco Núñez de Balboa, the first European to see the Pacific Ocean, had established a settlement there and sent back reports of abundant gold and an easy life for colonists. Pedrarias' expedition would increase the Spanish settlements and send this new source of wealth back to Spain.

In the beginning, de Soto was just another face among over 2,000 voyagers traveling on more than 20 ships for the New World. Their supplies included almost 200 tons of flour, 150 tons of biscuits and 69,000 gallons of oil and wine. Ships also carried materials for setting up new colonies, such as bells and crosses for new churches, beds and pharmaceutical supplies for new hospitals, chains and fetters for securing slaves, armor and weapons for soldiers, even young fruit trees and seeds for planting.

After several delays, the armada finally left Spain on April 11, 1514. De Soto left his boyhood behind and would not return to his homeland for 22 years.

After leaving Seville, the fleet made a brief stop at the Canary Islands for supplies and then anchored on June 3 off the shore of the Caribbean island of Dominica. A party of colonists went ashore to run errands and when one of them didn't follow orders, Governor Pedrarias, a harsh man and unforgiving disciplinarian who people obeyed out of fear, became enraged. He ordered the man hanged from a tree. Certainly, the lesson was a difficult one for the inexperienced teenager de Soto.

By the time most of the fleet arrived in Panama on June 26, de Soto probably was questioning the glorious stories he had heard about the New World. The settlement Balboa established consisted of shacks made from mud, bark and vines. Even less appealing was its location in a hot, humid and mosquito-infested area between a marshy beach and a dense jungle. To make matters worse, food was in short supply.

Besides the difficult living conditions, Pedrarias and Balboa got off to a poor start. Balboa was an explorer whose friendship with Indians enabled him to establish the settlement. Instead of accepting Balboa's inroads with Indians,

Pedrarias took a confrontational and impractical approach. Almost immediately, the new arrivals began brutal attacks on the native population, using their superior military equipment and training, vicious attack dogs that literally tore the Indians to pieces and other ferocious means.

Pedrarias eventually earned the well-deserved nickname of "Scourge of God." Some historians believe that as many as two million Indians died during his reign in Panama, including the Cueva tribe that became extinct within half a century of his arrival.

We know very little of de Soto during the first few years after his arrival. Gonzalo Fernández de Oviedo, another member of the expedition, wrote only that de Soto "was instructed in the school of Pedrarias Dávila, in the dissipation and devastation of the Indians. He was very occupied in the hunt to kill Indians."

De Soto learned another lesson in the "school of Pedrarias": in early 1519, despite giving one of his daughters to Balboa in marriage a couple of years earlier, Pedrarias imprisoned his son-in-law and beheaded him.

By then, de Soto and his two closest friends, Hernan Ponce de León and Francisco Campañón, had formed a partnership which would ultimately bring a great deal of wealth to all three men. He had also moved to a new community called Náta in the agricultural region of Parita. He lived there for several years, exploring the Central American isthmus and saving money he stole from Indians he tortured during expeditions.

Meanwhile, other Spanish explorers were exploring new areas of South and Central America. One was Gil González Dávila, who reached Nicaragua in 1522. He claimed the country was rich with powerful kings and palaces.

As news of Nicaragua spread, several conquistadors scrambled to beat González to whatever riches might lie in store there. Pedrarias organized an expedition in 1523 under the leadership of Francisco Hernández de Córdoba that de Soto joined. Córdoba was more interested in setting up cities than in plundering Indians. He established two cities in Nicaragua by the spring of 1524, Granada on Lake Nicaragua and the capital city of León. De Soto was among 33 founding members of León, north of Granada on Lake Managua. He was also among the first Europeans to cross Lake Nicaragua.

González double-crossed de Soto during a battle by promising to surrender. When de Soto laid down his arms, Gonzalez captured and disarmed him, then took his savings. The experience was one of de Soto's most humbling.

Later, Córdoba tried to take over Nicaragua for his own benefit. But de Soto was loyal to Pedrarias and opposed Córdoba, who threw the young man into prison. De Soto managed to escape and made his way back to Panama to inform Pedrarias of this betrayal. The governor responded with his usual fury. He sent another expedition to capture Córdoba and ordered the traitor's head to be chopped off.

De Soto, Ponce and Campañón formed a company in León that became one of the most successful in early colonial times. It included a mining operation in the Nueva Segovia Mountains, a shipping business with one of the largest vessels operating in the Pacific and an operation that provided slaves throughout the Spanish empire for half a decade. Nearly 2,000 Indian slaves worked the trio's land, mines and estates. Even though Campañón died in 1528, de Soto and Ponce continued to make money. But events several hundred miles to the south soon beckoned to de Soto's adventurous spirit.■

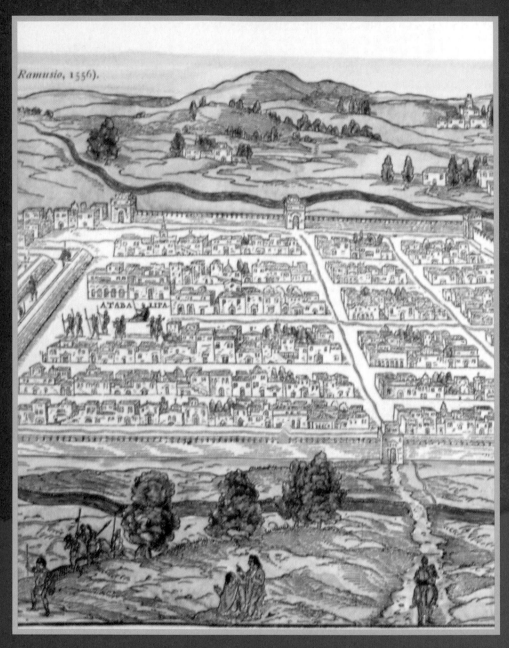

This hand-colored woodcut shows an Inca city in Peru in the 1550s. At the time, the Incas were one of the largest and richest civilizations in the Americas.

CONQUERING THE INCAS

Francisco Pizarro, another explorer from Extremadura and one of de Soto's first commanders in Panama, was hot on the trail of the immense wealth of the Incas, one of the largest and richest civilizations in the Americas. Their empire, called the Four Corners of the World or Tahuantinsuyu, stretched for more than 2,000 miles across what today is Peru, Ecuador and parts of Colombia, Bolivia, Chile and Argentina. A king who claimed to be the child of the sun ruled over nearly six million Indians living in the vast region. Some of the empire's accomplishments included roads linking distant provinces, a relay service for rapid messages and a mail service on the backs of llamas.

Pizarro had the support of Spain's King Charles I. He then sought de Soto's services as his second-in-command. Pedrarias, who had opposed Pizarro's explorations, ordered de Soto to stay where he was.

But when Pedrarias died suddenly in March 1531 at the age of 91, de Soto was free to join Pizarro. He recruited men and invested in two ships, horses and large quantities of food, arms and tools. Even so, Pizarro and de Soto together had less than 200 men to try to conquer a vast empire. But they were nothing if not daring.

After a long trek across a desert and through the Andes Mountains, the little army reached the city of Cajamarca. The Inca king Atahualpa and more than 30,000 warriors camped in tents on the outskirts. Pizarro sent de Soto and 15 men to meet Atahualpa.

As they entered the camp with trumpets blaring, de Soto dismounted from his horse, doffed his plumed helmet and approached the king, who was surrounded by nobles attired in rich robes, female servants and hundreds of armed warriors.

"Greetings, my lord," de Soto said. "I bring you the salutations of my governor, Don Francisco Pizarro, who earnestly wishes to pay his respects to you in person, in the name of our lord, the king of Spain."

Atahualpa sat cross-legged on a low stool and wore a tall golden crown with a tassel of red wool hanging on his forehead. He would not dignify de Soto's greeting with a response. Finally, one of the king's noblemen spoke up and said, "It is well."

Another lengthy silence followed. Again, a nobleman replied, "It is well," as the Spaniards waited in silence. Atahualpa finally broke his silence.

"Tell your captain that I am keeping a fast that will end tomorrow," the king commanded. "I will go and visit him with my captains. Meanwhile, he may go to the buildings on the square, and wait there until I arrive and ordain what should be done next."

De Soto knew Atahualpa was trying to intimidate him and he refused to show signs of weakness. Instead, he gave the king a taste of who he was up against. De Soto leaped into his saddle to flaunt his riding skills, concluding by riding so close to the king that his horse's breath stirred the fringe of red wool on Atahualpa's forehead.

Several of the king's men drew back in awe and later were sentenced to death for showing fear to strangers. Atahualpa himself did not flinch, but de Soto's display did pique the king's curiosity enough to converse with the Spaniards about wrongdoings they had committed since coming to his country. In one particularly horrific instance, de Soto and his men had raped 500 sacred virgins living in the Temple of the Sun in Cajas.

De Soto returned to Pizarro's camp with news about his meeting with Atahualpa and the leading Spaniards made a plan.

The next day, as the king made a spectacular entrance into the huge central plaza, carried on a litter and accompanied by thousands of retainers, there were no signs of anyone except a priest and an interpreter. The priest

Atahualpa, King of the Incas, would not dignify de Soto's greeting with a response.

handed Atahualpa a Bible, which he quickly threw to the ground. The priest yelled "Blasphemy!" as a signal for Spaniards to come out from hiding and attack. In the end, Pizarro's small army killed several thousand Incans and captured Atahualpa. The only Spanish casualty was Pizarro himself, who suffered a cut hand.

Pizarro promised Atahualpa that he would not harm him, and would release him once the king made good on his pledge to fill up the room where he was imprisoned with silver and gold. Indians spent seven months bringing in golden cups, pitchers, bowls, plates and masterpieces of art on the backs of llamas from every corner of the Inca empire. They stacked the riches nine feet high in a room 20 feet

This drawing shows Hernando de Soto in the camp of the Inca at Caxamalca. De Soto spent several years in the Inca Empire, fighting battles and leading an expedition to the Inca capital city of Cuzco.

long by 17 feet wide. They also filled another room twice with silver. The Spaniards then melted the riches into bars to facilitate dividing and transporting them. The ransom had an estimated value of nearly $100 million in today's money. It made Pizarro and de Soto among the richest men in the New World.

But wealth was not enough for the deceitful Pizarro. He feared Atahualpa would raise an Indian army against him so he executed the King on July 26, 1533 while de Soto was away on a mission. When de Soto returned, he was furious.

De Soto remained for two more years, fighting battles and leading an expedition to the Inca capital city of Cuzco, where he eventually became governor and enjoyed several adventures. He became the first horseman to cross the swaying bridges Indians made from willow stands. The bridges crossed gorges and chasms at dizzying heights in the Andes mountains.

He also had an affair with Tocto Chimpu, the daughter of an Inca prince and supposedly the most beautiful woman in Peru. They had a daughter Leonor, named after de Soto's mother, whose descendants carried on his name in Cuzco for several generations. But Leonor grew up not knowing her parents. De Soto left late in 1535 to return to Spain, and her mother died soon after. ■

In this illustration, de Soto finds Juan Ortiz living among the Indians. He was not Native American, but a survivor from the Pánfilo de Narváez expedition. He and three other Spaniards had fallen into the hands of Hirrihigua, who killed the other three. Ortiz was spared because the chief's wife and daughters begged that the teenager not be killed. Hirrihigua's daughter directed Ortiz to a neighboring village where Chief Mocozo welcomed him as one of the tribe. This is where de Soto first encountered Ortiz who became a trusted interpreter for him.

CHAPTER 4

A NEW CHALLENGE

De Soto, now wealthy beyond his wildest dreams, arrived in Spain early in 1536 and married Isabel de Bobadilla, the daughter of Pedrarias, in the Bobadilla family chapel in Valladolid that November. The king's whole court attended the lavish ceremony. Later, the newlyweds settled into a palace in Seville with a large courtyard, a grand staircase and numerous apartments on two floors.

At first, de Soto and Isabel were content just being together. But de Soto was still a young man in his mid-30s, and his adventurous spirit could not remain dormant for long. On his previous expeditions, he had served under other men. So now he asked the king, Charles I, to allow him to lead an expedition back to the New World in Ecuador. But the king was reluctant. He already had several powerful leaders in Central and South America, and didn't want to add another one. They could well end up fighting each other instead of working together to make Spain even richer.

But there was a huge, unexplored land to the north: Florida. It had been discovered in 1513 by Juan Ponce de León, and the land that Spanish called "La Florida" included not just the modern state but the entire southeastern part of the North American continent. Even though Ponce de León's expedition and a later one under Pánfilo de Narváez had ended in failure and the death of their leaders, de Soto was interested and began making preparations. King Charles raised him to a higher rank of nobility and named him governor of the colony of Cuba.

Then de Soto heard first-hand accounts from the famous explorer Alvar Núñez Cabeza de Vaca, who was one of only four survivors of the Narváez expedition. Cabeza de Vaca's stories about rich landscapes and prosperous settlements made de Soto even more excited about conquering the land himself.

He used his wealth to organize a large expedition, and nearly 1,000 Spaniards signed up to join him, including Isabel who originally did not support the idea. In April 1538, de Soto set sail for new horizons. He arrived in Cuba late the following month, but he wanted to make careful preparations. So he sent out several scouting expeditions to Florida while he waited in Cuba and assembled a powerful force of more than 600 men, 230 horses, some large dogs and even hundreds of hogs that the army would eat during their long journey. Finally he set out in mid-May of 1539, leaving Isabel behind in Cuba as acting governor. The post made her the first European woman to hold a high office in the Americas.

De Soto and his nine ships soon arrived off the coast of Florida, possibly near modern-day Tampa Bay. De Soto himself went ashore on May 29, and several days later, when all his men and horses had come ashore, he claimed the land in the name of the Spanish crown. De Soto was not in search of wealth as much this time as he had been in past expeditions. While finding gold and silver was important to him and to his men, he also wanted to explore the vast region to facilitate the establishment of settlements.

De Soto could not have imagined then that his men would eventually cover more than 3,000 miles through what are ten states today, including Florida, Georgia, South Carolina, North Carolina, Tennessee, Alabama, Mississippi, Arkansas, Louisiana and Texas. He could not have envisioned the Indian tribes he would encounter, nor the surprises that lay in store.

In the first big surprise a few days after landing, de Soto and his men came across a group of warriors wearing red war paint and feathers in tufts of hair on their heads. One of them ran forward wearing a loincloth and carrying a bow and arrow. He fell to his knees and made the sign of the cross saying, "In the name of God and the Blessed Virgin, do not kill me. I am a Christian."

The man was Juan Ortiz, a Spaniard from Seville who had been a member of the Narváez expedition. He had lived 12 years among Indians as a captive. In typical Spanish behavior toward the Indians, Narváez had cut off the nose of Hirrihigua, the local cacique, and killed the man's mother. Soon afterward, Ortiz and three others had fallen into the angry man's hands. He put them on a grill over an open fire, one by one. The three men died in horrible agony, and Ortiz, then a teenager, seemed destined for the same fate. But his screams made Hirrihigua's wife and daughters take pity on him, and they persuaded Hirrihigua to release the boy. Later, fearing that his life was still in danger, they took him to a neighboring tribe, where de Soto finally discovered him. De Soto was happy to let Ortiz join the expedition, and he became an indispensable translator because he knew several Indian languages.

We have four primary sources for what happened during the next few years. Three men who were part of de Soto's army—Rodrigo Ranjel, Luis Hernández de Biedma and a Portuguese known only as the Gentleman of Elvas—all kept journals. In addition, Garcilaso de la Vega, also known as "the Inca" because his mother was an Inca and his father a Spaniard, was born the year that de Soto landed in Florida. He became interested in the expedition as he grew older and interviewed several of the survivors to write his account. While these four accounts all differ in many of their specifics, the overall picture they describe is very similar. So we have a pretty good idea of what took place.

As de Soto was quick to learn, Florida was not Panama. Nor was it the Inca Empire. These Indians were not going to just roll over, and he encountered problems almost from the beginning. While he often tried to bargain with local tribes, the Spanish already had a well-deserved reputation for being cruel, a reputation that de Soto would add to during the next few years. Because his army was so powerful, the Indians wouldn't confront his men in the open combat that Spanish soldiers were used to. Instead they hid in the shadows, firing arrows and vanishing into the surrounding forest. That forced the men to wear their armor and heavy quilted clothing for protection in the hot Florida sun.

What was worse, de Soto didn't find any gold. And his men were often hungry. Sometimes, they would find villages that had been abandoned by Indians who were afraid of them. They would take whatever food they could find, which made the Indians angry.

Finally, in mid-September, 1539, they entered the village of Napituca, which is probably near today's Gainesville. The cacique of the village, Vitacucho, prepared a feast for the tired men. But Ortiz overheard plans for a surprise attack and forewarned de Soto.

Vitacucho later invited de Soto to watch his warriors parade in a nearby meadow. De Soto accepted and told Vitacucho, "My men will march side by side with your men." De Soto and his men followed Vitacucho to the field where they met the warriors—we don't know how many as Biedma says 300-400 while the Inca gives a figure of 10,000— covered in war paint and armed for battle. Vitacucho then raised his hatchet in the air as a signal to begin fighting, and the two sides lit into one another. After months of fighting shadowy figures who hid behind trees, the Spaniards were happy to fight in an open field. They quickly killed many Indians using their long lances and drove many more into a broad pond where Spaniards surrounded them. The water was so deep they had to lift one another up to shoot their arrows.

De Soto told them he would spare their lives if they surrendered, but the Indians continued fighting for at least fourteen hours. Finally, they came to shore exhausted, with many begging to be killed because they could not bear the shame of being defeated in battle. Instead, de Soto took them captive. But when he was sharing a meal with them the next day, one of them struck him in the face while the others fought to escape. Many Indians were killed in the struggle, and some who survived were executed afterward.

The Spanish continued their march, and arrived the following month at a village called Anhaica, near modern-day Tallahassee, where they spent the winter. It was close to the coastline, so the remaining ships were able to anchor nearby.

Eventually the men heard exciting news. A kingdom named Cofitachequi that was ruled by a woman lay to the northeast, and it contained gold, silver and precious pearls. They eagerly awaited the coming of better weather so they could march there.■

This hand-colored engraving shows de Soto taking several Indians captive and forcing them to accompany him on his march.

GOOD TIMES

Before leaving Anhaica in March, 1540, de Soto ordered the ships to return to Cuba. He directed them to meet him that fall with additional men and supplies in the Bay of Achuse, which is probably modern-day Mobile Bay, some 100 miles further west. Everyone felt confident that they would rendezvous laden with treasure. But as the ships disappeared over the horizon, no one could imagine that this would be the last news of de Soto for more than three years.

On their way north, the expedition passed through present-day Georgia into South Carolina. After two months on the march, exhausted and half-starved, they finally found the village of Cofitachequi. The cacica turned out to be the most hospitable Indian they met, and the grateful Spaniards called her La Señora de Cofitachequi after meeting her on the Watcree River near Lugoff, South Carolina in early May, 1540.

She was dressed in soft white cotton and wore a crown of eagle feathers. Much more important to the tired Spaniards, who often had to fight their way into Indian villages, she invited them to stay with her. She sent half her villagers away to provide room for her guests and also offered to share the tribe's limited supply of food. But to de Soto's great disappointment, the "gold" he had looked forward to finding turned out to be copper and the "silver" was mica. But she did have something else of value: pearls. De Soto took several baskets full of pearls for himself, and allowed all the men to put an additional two handfuls into their packs.

Once the men got over their initial disappointment at finding no precious metals, they began to enjoy the pleasant living conditions so much that many of them wanted to remain and found a colony. It was located in an area that appeared to be suitable for agriculture, and even more important, it wasn't far from the sea. The plentiful pearls would be valuable trading commodities.

But de Soto declined. He was a man on the march. Rumors of yet more gold drove him onward. So less than two weeks after his arrival, he ordered the men to pack up.

"Although it seemed a mistake to leave that land, no one had anything to say to him after his determination was learned," wrote the Gentleman of Elvas.

De Soto repaid La Señora for her kindness and hospitality by kidnapping her, forcing her and some villagers to accompany them on the march, though eventually they escaped. Soon afterward, the expedition crossed the Appalachian mountain range—the first Europeans to accomplish that feat—then turned south into Tennessee, western Georgia and modern-day Alabama.

That summer of 1540 was perhaps the most pleasant part of the entire expedition. For weeks on end, the marching tactics they had developed worked well. The Indians, who by now had heard of the mysterious and powerful strangers, were willing to cooperate to rid themselves of the invaders as soon as possible. For the Spaniards, the system insured leisurely marches, ample Indians to carry their baggage, plenty of food, and almost no risk of danger from attack. Each day brought de Soto about 12 miles closer to his planned meeting with his returning ships in Achuse Bay. Perhaps he planned on establishing a base of operations there, then returning to the most promising areas to found further colonies.

As de Soto approached the kingdom of Tascalusa, he probably envisioned another easy crossing through the territory of an Indian who wouldn't cause any problems. So when he met Tascalusa in person, he made the usual demands: baggage carriers, food, females.

At first the Indian, one of the most powerful caciques they would meet during the entire expedition, refused. De Soto quickly put him under close guard. So Tascalusa partly agreed to de Soto's demands, by supplying him with 400 men to carry the baggage. He said that everything else de Soto demanded would be waiting—at Mabila. So they set off for the town, a week's travel away, with Tascalusa still guarded. According to all accounts, Tascalusa was a huge man, perhaps as tall as six and a half feet. His moccasins may have nearly brushed the ground as he rode one of de Soto's pack horses.

As the army proceeded slowly along the Alabama river, two Spaniards were killed—the first deaths mentioned in six months. The enraged de Soto told Tascalusa that he would burn him alive unless he turned over the Indians who were responsible.

The chief gave him the same reply: "At Mabila."

De Soto had no idea that that simple phrase was the death knell of his hopes for his expedition. ■

De Soto was certainly not the first person to stand on the shore of the Mississippi, but he was most likely the first European to cross the river.

THE MIGHTY MISSISSIPPI

After the battle, the Spanish stayed in the vicinity of Mabila for nearly a month. During this time, de Soto learned that his ships were where he had ordered them to be, less than 80 miles away. He faced a difficult choice. He could march directly to the ships, board them and sail back to Cuba and reorganize, coming back to La Florida with an even larger expedition.

The problem was that if he returned now, with many of his men still wounded and—far more importantly—without any treasure now that their pearls had burned up in Mabila, the chances of ever returning would be minimal. Perhaps the king would take away his right to explore Florida and give it to someone else. He might even be replaced as governor of Cuba.

Or he could return to the ships, take the supplies that they brought and establish a base of operations as he may have planned all along. But after Mabila, some of the men were complaining. They had been in La Florida for more

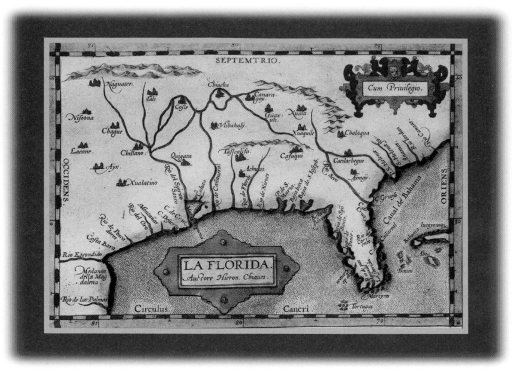

This somewhat inaccurate map of Florida was created by Christopher Plantino in 1588, some years after de Soto's exploration of the area. Note that what was called Florida was most of the southeastern part of the United States. Some historians believe that "La Florida" was the Spanish term for North America at that time.

than a year, with nothing to show for it. If they arrived at the ships, many might simply demand to be taken back to Cuba.

De Soto made up his mind. Though his men had very little clothing and few weapons apart from what they had finished the battle with, he swung north and began searching for a suitable place to spend his second winter in the New World. He didn't even send word to the anxiously waiting ships of his decision.

After a month of traveling, the Spanish settled down for the winter in an abandoned village in the territory belonging to Chickasaw Indians. Over the next few months, the relations between the two sides grew worse.

Again de Soto miscalculated. Despite the likelihood of an attack, he didn't make adequate defensive preparations, so hostile warriors crept in and launched a dawn attack in March, 1541. The Spanish were caught by surprise, and suffered heavy losses: a dozen men and many of their valuable horses. The village was burned down, and most of their remaining clothing and many weapons were destroyed. Had the Indians pressed their advantage, they might have been able to annihilate the entire expedition.

But the Chickasaws hesitated. Though they shivered in the chilly nights, the Spanish were able to rebuild their weapons. When the Indians attacked again the following week, de Soto and his men were ready. They drove their attackers away with minimal losses.

The expedition headed west. Soon they encountered an Indian roadblock. Though his men argued against a confrontation, de Soto disregarded them. Fifteen more dead Spaniards paid the price for their leader's stubbornness, though the Indians eventually retreated. By this time, de Soto appears to have had little purpose or direction. His army was acting much like a wounded animal, striking out blindly.

A few weeks later, on what is likely May 8th, 1541, they encountered what de Soto is most associated with today: the Mississippi River. Historians are not sure of the exact location, but a likely place is Commerce Landing in northwestern Mississippi, just south of the Tennessee border. The river presented a formidable barrier. It was well over a mile wide and had swift, swirling currents. In addition, large canoes full of Indians with bows and arrows appeared unwilling to allow the Spaniards to make an uncontested crossing.

De Soto's men rigged up four large rafts with oars and crude sails, and crossed the Mississippi River early on June

18, 1541, successfully evading the Indians. After landing in modern-day Arkansas, they continued marching north where they encountered a large Casqui village. The chief thought de Soto was a god.

"We know you are the Children of the Sun," the chief told Spaniards. "Your weapons are more powerful than ours, and so must your religion be. Our newly sown fields are in need of water. Ask your God for rain, and we will worship him."

De Soto indulged the chief by ordering the building of a pine cross on top of a hill. Later, Spanish priests blessed the cross, and thousands of Indians arrived to witness the strange ceremony. The next day storm clouds rolled in, and the sky opened up on the parched fields much to the joy of Indians and Spaniards alike.

But this was one of the few occasions for joy for de Soto. Increasingly desperate, he sent out men on scouting expeditions, still hoping to discover gold. None were successful.

The Mississippi presented a formidable barrier to de Soto and his men, and the Indians were unwilling to let the Spaniards make an uncontested crossing.

All too soon it was time to look for winter quarters, now for the third time. Several of the writers suggest that de Soto had developed a plan: the following spring he would send a ship down the Mississippi and back to Cuba, where it would not only provide news of him to his anxiously waiting wife— who had heard almost nothing of him since his departure— but also provide an opportunity to refit and reorganize his expedition and press even further west. He still remembered the glowing reports that Cabeza de Vaca had provided.

But completely unknown to him, another Spanish expedition, this one under the command of Francisco Vásquez de Coronado, had been inflamed by the same reports. Coronado's expedition had left Mexico early in 1540 and explored the American Southwest. By mid-1541, the expedition had penetrated eastward as far as Kansas. At one point, the two groups were slightly less than 300 miles from each other, though neither had the slightest idea of the other's existence. But in both cases, their search for gold produced the same result: Nothing.

The men settled in for a third winter after several months of aimless wandering in Arkansas. Unfortunately, the translator Ortiz died and his loss made it even more difficult to communicate with the local Indians. The Spaniards returned to the Mississippi River in the spring of 1542.

Probably they were trying to find a place where they could spend a few quiet months, building small ships that would carry some or all the remaining men back to Cuba. In one final effort to impress the local Indians with his power, de Soto sent some men into an unsuspecting Indian village. The Spaniards attacked just after dawn and killed more than 100 villagers. ■

This woodcut is copied from a painting entitled Midnight Mass of the Mississippi Over the Body of Ferdinand [Hernando] De Soto, by Edward Moran, 1898. De Soto was buried at sea to keep the Native Americans from digging up his grave.

THE DEATH OF DE SOTO

B y now, de Soto was a seriously ill man. In all likelihood, he caught malaria from mosquitoes living in the surrounding swamps. Malaria is a disease that causes chills, fever and sweating and can eventually kill its host.

His fever got so high by mid-May that he could not walk or stand. He called his men together, named Luis Moscoso as the expedition's new leader and finally asked them to leave him alone with a priest for a final confession. He died May 21, 1542. He was probably 42 years old.

In the will he wrote just before leaving Cuba in 1539, he left elaborate instructions for his burial and set aside a large sum of money to build a chapel and tomb in his boyhood church of San Miguel in Jerez de los Caballeros. But the reality was quite a bit different. He was at least 3,000 miles away from the place of his birth in an era when there was no practical way of preserving corpses.

And there was a more pressing reason why his wishes were disregarded. Amid the sadness of de Soto's death, his men feared that their leader's absence would make them vulnerable among Indians who thought he was immortal. They did not want to bury him near the river for fear that Indians might discover his grave. So they placed de Soto's body inside a heavy oak log (or perhaps they just wrapped him in a blanket and filled it with stones) so that it would sink, put the coffin in a canoe at night and then slid it into the deepest part of the river.

With that sad task behind them, the Spaniards decided to make a quick exit before the Indians learned their secret. They tried at first to reach Mexico by marching more than 400 miles across Arkansas and Texas. But eventually the terrain lying in front of them became barren and deserted, so they turned back to the Mississippi River. There they spent several months constructing seven boats with awkward sails made from leather and what was left of their cloaks. Then they had to battle their way downriver to the Gulf of Mexico. After several more weeks, they arrived at a Spanish settlement in Mexico. Their journey finally came to an end in the fall of 1543, more than four years after they set out and long after they had been given up for dead. About half the survivors decided to return to Spain.

For the most part, Hernando de Soto's expedition had ended in failure. He didn't find gold. He didn't establish any settlements. He converted few Indians to the Christian faith. His harsh treatment of the Indians would make things more difficult for future explorers. And it cost him his life.

Even the credit for his most famous "discovery"—the Mississippi River—probably belongs to someone else. A Spanish explorer named Alvarez de Pineda sailed from Jamaica in 1519 in an effort to find the passage that people during that era believed made Florida an island. Of course, there is no such passage, but as Pineda sailed along the Gulf Coast he apparently came across the Mississippi as it flows into the Gulf of Mexico, and may have even sailed up to 20 miles upriver.

But almost certainly de Soto was the first European to cross the river, and for nearly two years it was the most important geographical feature for his expedition, eventually providing the means of escape for its survivors.

In addition, the chroniclers left behind an invaluable glimpse of Indian life before it was forever changed in the years to come as Europeans began swarming over the land.

De Soto left behind one very interesting historical question: What if his expedition had been successful? A colony in South Carolina, Mobile Bay or on the banks of the Mississippi could have paved the way for Spain to gain a major foothold in this country decades before the English landed Jamestown and Plymouth Rock. In that case, the entire history of this country would have been very different. ■

In the winter of 1543, survivors of de Soto's expedition returned to the Mississippi to find their way back to Mexico. They built seven large boats. Hostile Indians pursued them and 12 of the remaining men were drowned.

CHRONOLOGY

ca. 1500 born in Jerez de los Caballeros in the province of Extremadura, Spain to Francisco Méndez de Soto and Leonor Arias Tinoco

1514   leaves Spain for the New World under the leadership of Don Pedrarias Dávila, governor of Darién in what is Panama today

1519   moves to town of Natá in western Panama

1523   explores Nicaragua under the leadership of Francisco Hernández de Córdoba

1531   joins Pizarro in Peru as his second in command after Pedrarias dies

1536   returns to Spain and marries Isabel de Bobadilla

1537   receives permission to outfit an expedition to Florida from King Charles I of Spain, who also appoints him governor of Cuba

1538   departs with fleet from Spain for Cuba

1539   goes to Florida and leaves Isabel behind in Cuba as acting governor

1540   fights battle of Mabila, Alabama

1541   reaches and crosses the Mississippi River

1542   dies from malaria on the western bank of the Mississippi River

TIMELINE IN HISTORY

1492   Christopher Columbus becomes the first European to reach the Americas
1506   Columbus dies
1513   Juan Ponce de León discovers Florida; Vasco Núñez de Balboa becomes the first European to see the Pacific Ocean
1516   King Ferdinand II of Spain dies
1519   Ferdinand Magellan begins round-the-world voyage; Pedrarias executes Balboa
1521   Ponce de León's second voyage to Florida ends with his death after being wounded by an Indian arrow; Hernando Cortés conquers Mexico's Aztec Indians
1522   Gil González Dávila becomes the first European to find Nicaragua and Lake Nicaragua
1524   Pizarro begins four-year exploration in Ecuador and Peru
1526   Lucas Vázquez de Ayllon tries to found colony on the South Carolina coast with 600 men, women and children
1528   Pánfilo de Narváez begins exploration of Florida, but his expedition is wrecked; Pizarro sails to Spain with evidence of potential riches in Peru to try to persuade the king to grant him the authority to conquer the country
1531   Pizarro returns to Peru
1532   Pizarro conquers the Incas and executes their ruler, King Atahualpa, the following year
1536   Álvar Núñez Cabeza de Vaca and three other men, the only survivors of Narváez' expedition, are discovered in Mexico
1540   Francisco Vázquez de Coronado begins exploration of American Southwest that eventually extends as far as modern-day Kansas
1541   Pizarro is assassinated
1543   de Soto's remaining men travel down the Mississippi River to Mexico via the Gulf of Mexico
1565   Pedro Menéndez de Avilés establishes St. Augustine, Florida, which becomes oldest US city
1607   Jamestown colony founded
1620   Pilgrims land at Plymouth Rock

FOR FURTHER READING

Albornoz, Miguel. *Hernando de Soto: Knight of the Americas.* Translated from the Spanish by Bruce Boeglin. New York: Franklin Watts, 1986.

Brown, Virginia Pounds. *Cochula's Journey.* Montgomery, AL: Black Belt Press, 1996.

Carson, Robert. *The World's Great Explorers: Hernando De Soto.* Chicago: Childrens Press, Inc., 1991.

Chrisman, Abbott. *Hernando de Soto.* Austin, TX: Raintree Streck-Vaughn, 1993.

Duncan, David Ewing. *Hernando de Soto: A Savage Quest in the Americas.* New York: Crown Publishers, Inc., 1996.

Gallagher, Jim. *Hernando de Soto and the Exploration of Florida.* Philadelphia: Chelsea House Publishers, 2000.

Hemming, John. *The Conquest of the Incas.* New York: Harcourt, Brace, 1970.

Hodge, Frederick Webb and Theodore H. Lewis, eds. *Spanish Explorers in the Southern United States, 1528-1543.* Austin, TX: Texas State Historical Association, 1984.

Hudson, Joyce Rockwood. *Looking for De Soto: A Search Through the South for the Spaniard's Trail.* Athens, GA: University of Georgia Press, 1993.

Maynard, Theodore. *De Soto and the Conquistadores.* New York: AMS Press, 1978.

Montgomery, Elizabeth Rider. *A World Explorer: Hernando De Soto.* Champaign, IL: Garrard Publishing Co., 1964.

Swanton, John R. *Final Report of the United States de Soto Expedition Commission.* Washington, DC: Smithsonian Institution Press, 1985.

Syme, Ronald. *De Soto: Finder of the Mississippi.* New York: William Morrow & Co., 1957.

Thompson, Kathleen and Jan Gleiter. *Hernando de Soto.* Milwaukee, WI: Raintree Publishers, 1989.

Vega, Garcilaso de la. *The Fabulous De Soto Story: The Florida of the Inca.* Translated and edited by John G. Varner and Jeanette J. Varner. Austin, TX: The University of Texas Press, 1951.

ON THE WEB

De Soto's Trail through the Southeast
www. conquestchannel.com/inset7.html
Letters on Texas Explorers: de Soto
www.rice.edu/armadillo/Projects/desoto.html
The Soto Expedition
www.archeologyinc.org/soto.html

GLOSSARY

armada (ar-MAH-duh)—a large group or force, such as ships or airplanes

blasphemy (BLAS-fuh-mee)—acting disrespectfully toward God or sacred things

buckler —a round shield with a grip for holding, and sometimes with straps through which the arm is passed

cacica (kuh-SEE-kuh)—female chief of a Native American tribe

cacique (kuh-SEEK)—male chief of a Native American tribe

chivalry (SHIV-ul-ree)—qualities expected of a knight, including courage, generosity and courtesy

chroniclers (KRON-ih-klurs)—people who write about historical events, often from first-hand knowledge

colonist—inhabitant of a settlement in a new land that another country oversees

conquistador (kahn-KEES-tuh-door)—one of the 16th century Spanish conquerors in the Americas

friar—member of a religious order, especially the Franciscans and Dominicans

halberd—a shafted weapon with an ax-like cutting blade, beak and spike used in the 15th and 16th centuries

impale—to pierce with a sharpened stake trust through the body for torture or punishment

interpreter—person who translates words from one language to another

knell (NELL)—mournful sound that signals sorrow

knight (NIGHT)—a man, usually of noble birth, who was raised to an honorable military rank and bound to chivalrous conduct

litter—a vehicle suspended by shafts and carried by men or animals with a bed or couch on top and often covered and curtained

malaria—a disease characterized by attacks of chills, fever and sweating and caused by parasites that are transferred to the human bloodstream where they destroy red blood cells

molten—liquefied by heat, in a state of fusion

Moor—a Muslim of the mixed Berber and Arab people from northwest Africa

Muslim—an adherent of Islam, a religious faith that teaches Allah is the only God, Mohammed is his prophet and the Koran is a sacred text

palisade (pal-ih-SAYD)—fence made of high wooden stakes that surrounds a village or town to protect it from enemies

porter—person who carries baggage

ransom—the payment of a demanded valuable to release from captivity

pelt—the hide or skin of an animal

plunder—to rob of goods or valuables by open force, as in war or hostile raids

province—an administrative division or unit in a country such as Spain, similar to states in the US

scourge (SKURJ)—a person or thing who harasses or destroys

treason— violation of the allegiance one owes to his government or ruler

INDEX